THE POCKET
CHÖGYAM TRUNGPA

THE POCKET CHÖGYAM TRUNGPA

Compiled and Edited by
CAROLYN ROSE GIMIAN

SHAMBHALA
Boston & London
2008

Shambhala Publications, Inc.
Horticultural Hall
300 Massachusetts Avenue
Boston, MA 02115
www.shambhala.com

© 2008 by Diana J. Mukpo
This book is an abridged edition of *Ocean of Dharma*,
published by Shambhala Publications in 2008.
Cover photo: Photographer unknown,
from the collection of the Shambhala Archives.

9   8   7   6   5   4   3   2   1

First Edition
Printed in China
This edition is printed on acid-free paper that meets the
American National Standards Institute z39.48 Standard.

Distributed in the United States by Random House, Inc.,
and in Canada by Random House of Canada Ltd.

Library of Congress Cataloging-in-Publication Data

Trungpa, Chögyam, 1939–1987.
The pocket Chögyam Trungpa / compiled and edited by
Carolyn Rose Gimian.—1st ed.
        p.   cm.
Abridged ed. of *Ocean of dharma*. Shambhala, 2008.
Includes bibliographical references.
ISBN 978-1-59030-643-7 (pbk.: alk. paper)
1. Trungpa, Chögyam, 1939–1987—Quotations. 2. Spiritual life—
Buddhism—Quotations, maxims, etc. I. Gimian, Carolyn Rose
II. Trungpa, Chögyam, 1939–1987. Ocean of dharma. III. Title.
BQ990.R867A25   2008
294.3'4432—dc22
                                    2008015066

CONTENTS

EDITOR'S INTRODUCTION

IT SEEMS as if everywhere we look these days we see violence and suffering. Though we might wish that things were different, fulfilling our desires for a more peaceful and happy life, in fact we must live in *this* world, not the world of our dreams. Full of speed, passion, anger, many defeats, and few victories, nevertheless, the world as it is gives us much to celebrate. The kindness and courage of human beings, the awesome beauty of nature, the spark of intelligence and goodness that will not be extinguished—we also cannot deny these elements of life. And there is much to be done to help ourselves and to help this world, if we are willing. That is the essential message and the wisdom that permeates *The Pocket Chögyam Trungpa.*

This book of 108 short quotations is drawn from the writings of Chögyam Trungpa, the renowned Tibetan Buddhist teacher whose books transformed the understanding of Buddhism in the West. Virtually everyone now practicing the dharma in North America has been influenced, knowingly or not, by Chögyam Trungpa Rinpoche and his presentation of the Buddhist teachings. ("Rinpoche" is a title given to revered reincarnate lamas.)

Chögyam Trungpa had a passionate belief in the workability of our everyday lives. Life may present us with many problems, but he showed that it also offers us a genuine journey and many small wonders to appreciate. He taught that spirituality was not about becoming someone else but about becoming fully yourself and becoming completely engaged with your experience. He looked directly at many of the tough issues in life, such as aggression, fear, suffering, depression, and loneliness. In many of his teachings he also seemed to be looking ahead at what the challenges in the future might be. He spoke extensively about the interplay of fear and fearlessness, the need for a path of nonaggressive spiritual warriorship, and the dangers of spiritual and psychological materialism—and he foresaw many of the thorniest problems that would face society as well as the individual.

Trungpa Rinpoche's views were based not only on the ancient wisdom of his tradition but also on his own contemporary experience, his examination of life, and on his ability to predict how situations might evolve in the future. He appreciated paradox and the ironic contradictions of modern life. He thought that confusion and chaos were workable; in fact, viewed properly, they could be extremely good news.

Born and educated in Tibet, Trungpa Rinpoche saw his culture devastated by the communist Chinese invasion of 1959. Following his escape from Tibet, he studied at Oxford University and acquired a prodigious English vocabulary and uncanny understanding of Western culture and mind. He arrived in North America in 1970 and remained there until his death, teaching extensively and establishing many dharma centers and other institutions such as Naropa University and Shambhala Training.

He presented the buddhadharma in English, a savvy and sophisticated speaker of the language. (As one of his editors for more than thirty years, I—a native English speaker—have learned many new English words from him, encountered in his books and lectures.) The vocabulary that Chögyam Trungpa shaped for Buddhism in America has already entered the mainstream in a number of cases. His use of the word *ego* as a translation for the Sanskrit *atman,* is quoted in the *Oxford English Dictionary,* for instance. Unique phrases he coined like *spiritual materialism, meditation-in-action,* and *crazy wisdom* are now routinely used in Buddhist parlance.

The Pocket Chögyam Trungpa brings together quotations from his work that I hope will speak to a broad readership. I have searched for material that can be readily understood without an extensive background in Buddhist philosophy or practice. I would not claim to be finding *the* quotes that will become popular in the culture. There are so many possibilities; it's hard to know which ones will prove to be the most compelling. Reading Trungpa Rinpoche's work at a micro level, sentence by sentence or paragraph by paragraph, one sees his genius. The appeal is based on more than the craft of language. In just a few words, one senses a profound level of understanding and accomplishment, as well as concern for human welfare and indeed for all sentient beings, and one feels a deep reservoir of love and a sparkling humor that bursts out in unexpected ways.

Some of the quotes presented here deal with experiences that are inspired by or arise from the sitting practice of meditation, which is common to a great number of schools of Buddhism. Although details of the practice vary from one school to another, the similarities are such that I believe that the quotations in this volume apply universally. For those curious about meditation but untutored in the technique, an introduction to the practice of meditation is offered at the end of the book.

In one of his writings, Chögyam Trungpa says that anyone who creates a work of art has to meditate, whether they call the activity meditation or not. Wherever one finds a gap or a sense of space in life, whatever it is that one does that provides a feeling of ground, earth, or being—fundamentally, that is meditation. With that in mind, I think that almost anyone could connect with the material in this book.

I believe that Chögyam Trungpa would have been very pleased by the publication of this book. He told a number of his students that he would like a pocket book of short quotations from his Buddhist teachings to be published, one literally small enough to fit in the breast pocket of a shirt. Here it is, at last!

Chögyam Trungpa was a very genuine teacher, and as such he didn't just teach to please people. However, he did always teach to help others and to wake them up. Sometimes the sea is cold and turbulent; sometimes its waters are warm and soothing. In the ocean of dharma, the sense of transformation may not always be pleasant—growth usually involves some discomfort. I hope, however, that you will find your swim refreshing.

Carolyn Rose Gimian

ACKNOWLEDGMENTS

CHÖGYAM TRUNGPA's first book in English, his autobiography *Born in Tibet,* was published in 1966. More than forty years later, the manuscripts, audio recordings, and transcripts of his dharma talks continue to be edited and transformed into books, which now number more than three dozen. I would like to thank the many editors of his work, particularly Judith Lief and Sherab Chödzin Kohn, as well as an army of volunteers and a few dedicated staff people who have recorded, archived, restored, and transcribed his voice. The Shambhala Archives deserves thanks for preserving all of the original recordings of Chögyam Trungpa's lectures. My thanks for allowing extensive access to their collections.

The Pocket Chögyam Trungpa is abridged from *Ocean of Dharma: The Everyday Wisdom of Chögyam Trungpa.* That volume is drawn in part from quotations posted to the Ocean of Dharma Listserv (http://ocean ofdharma.com), through which I send out short teachings by Trungpa Rinpoche several times a week. I would like to thank the staff at Shambhala Publications who so ably administer the list, particularly Lenny Jacobs, and all of the Ocean of Dharma subscribers, who provide ideas for quotes, feedback on material, and often encouragement.

Since 1969, Shambhala Publications has been the publisher for the vast majority of the books by Chögyam Trungpa, and they continue to support the publication of new work. I have had the pleasure of working with several Shambhala editors, all of whom I thank for their contributions to shaping the work of Chögyam Trungpa. I would like to thank Sam and Hazel Bercholz, founders of Shambhala Publications, and now Sara Bercholz, for their commitment to this important body of dharma teachings. Particular thanks also to Peter Turner, the president of Shambhala Publications, for his guidance and support of our publishing program; and Eden Steinberg for her constant editorial ministrations; as well as Ben Gleason, Lora Zorian, and Daniel Urban, who all have had a hand in this book.

Deepest thanks as well to Diana J. Mukpo, Sakyong Mipham Rinpoche, and the Mukpo family, who continue to support and further Chögyam Trungpa's legacy and the publication of his work.

And of course, to the grandmaster himself, a deep bow of gratitude for these teachings and the opportunity to work with them.

Carolyn Rose Gimian

THE POCKET
CHÖGYAM TRUNGPA

A GOOD JOURNEY

OUR LIFE is an endless journey. It is like a broad highway that extends infinitely into the distance. The practice of meditation provides a vehicle to travel on that road. Our journey consists of constant ups and downs, hope and fear, but it is a good journey. The practice of meditation allows us to experience all the textures of the roadway, which is what the journey is all about. Through the practice of meditation, we begin to find that within ourselves there is no fundamental complaint about anything or anyone at all.

THE EMOTIONAL UMBILICAL CORD

FROM THE moment you are born, when you first cry and breathe free from your mother's womb, you are a separate individual. Of course, there is still emotional attachment, or an emotional umbilical cord, that connects you to your parents, but as you grow older and pass from infancy into youth and maturity, as each year passes, your attachment decreases. You become an individual who can function separate from your mother and father. Individuals can develop personal discipline so that they become mature and independent and therefore experience a sense of personal freedom. But then, once that development has taken place, it is equally important to share the comradeship of human society. This is an organic expression of the greater vision of warriorship. It is based on the appreciation of a larger world.

3

WHAT IS A WARRIOR?

A NYONE WHO is interested in hearing the dharma, anyone who is interested in finding out about oneself, and anyone who is interested in practicing meditation is basically a warrior. The approach of cowardice is looking for some tremendous external help, whether it comes from the sky or from the earth. You are afraid of actually seeing yourself; therefore you use spirituality or religion as a seeming way of seeing yourself without looking directly at yourself at all. Basically, when people are embarrassed about themselves, there's no fearlessness involved. Therefore, anybody who is interested in looking at oneself, finding out about oneself, and practicing on the spot could be regarded as a warrior.

4

FACING OURSELVES

WE HAVE a fear of facing ourselves. That is the obstacle. Experiencing the innermost core of our existence is very embarrassing to a lot of people. A lot of people turn to something that they hope will liberate them without their having to face themselves. That is impossible. We can't do that. We have to be honest with ourselves. We have to see our gut, our excrement, our most undesirable parts. We have to see them. That is the foundation of warriorship, basically speaking. Whatever is there, we have to face it, we have to look at it, study it, work with it, and practice meditation with it.

5

OUR HUMAN ENDOWMENT

PEOPLE OFTEN talk about trying to hold back their tears, but as human beings, we should take pride in our capacity to be sad and happy. We mustn't ignore the preciousness of our human birth or take it for granted. It is extremely precious and very powerful. We cannot ignore our basic human endowment.

6

CREATIVE
REVOLUTION

BUDDHA WAS a great revolutionary in his way of thinking. He even denied the existence of Brahma, or God, the creator of the world. He determined to accept nothing which he had not first discovered for himself. This does not mean to say that he disregarded the great and ancient tradition of India. He respected it very much. His was not an anarchistic attitude in any negative sense, nor was it revolutionary in the way the communists are. His was real, positive revolution. He developed the creative side of revolution, which is not trying to get help from anyone else, but finding out for oneself. By developing such a revolutionary attitude one learns a great deal.

7

THE STARTING POINT

IT WOULD be foolish to study more advanced subjects before we are familiar with the starting point, the nature of ego. Speculations about the goal become mere fantasy. These speculations may take the form of advanced ideas and descriptions of spiritual experiences, but they only exploit the weaker aspects of human nature, our expectations and desires to see and hear something colorful, something extraordinary. If we begin our study with these dreams of extraordinary, "enlightening," and dramatic experiences, then we will build up our expectations and preconceptions so that later, when we are actually working on the path, our minds will be occupied largely with what will be rather than with what is. It is destructive and not fair to people to play on their weaknesses, their expectations and dreams, rather than to present the realistic starting point of what they are. It is necessary, therefore, to start on what we are and why we are searching.

8

UNDOING
HABITUAL PATTERNS

IN ORDER to overcome ego, we have to undo our habitual patterns, which we have been developing for thousands of years, thousands of eons, up to this point. Such habitual patterns may not have any realistic ground, but nonetheless, we have been accustomed to doing their dirty work, so to speak. We are used to our habitual patterns and neuroses at this point. We have been used to them for such a long time that we end up believing they are the real thing. In order to overcome that, to begin with, we have to see our egolessness: seeing the egolessness of oneself and the

egolessness of other, and how we can actually overcome our anxiety and pain, which
in Buddhist terms is known as freedom,
liberation, freedom from anxiety. That is
precisely what nirvana means—relief.

BUDDHA IS
EVERYWHERE

Buddha can't be avoided. Buddha is everywhere. Enlightenment possibilities are all over the place. Whether you're going to get married tomorrow, whether you're going to die tomorrow, whatever you may feel, that familiar awake quality is everywhere, all the time. From this point of view, everything is a footprint of Buddha, anything that goes on, whether we regard it as sublime or ridiculous. Everything we do—breathing, farting, getting mosquito bites, having fantastic ideas about reality, thinking clever thoughts, flushing the toilet—whatever occurs is a footprint.

CHAOS IS THE
INSPIRATION

VERY BEAUTIFUL situations have developed using chaos as part of the enlightened approach. There is chaos of all kinds developing all the time: psychological disorder, social disorder, metaphysical disorder, or physical disorder, constantly happening. If you are trying to stop those situations, you are looking for external means of liberating yourself, another answer. But if we are able to look into the basic situation, then chaos is the inspiration, confusion is the inspiration.

THE BUDDHA AND BASIC GOODNESS

BUDDHISTS TRY to follow the example of the Buddha. The Buddha was an Indian prince who decided to abandon his palace and his kingdom in order to find out what life is all about. He was looking for the meaning of life, the purpose of life. He wanted to know who and what he was. So he went and practiced meditation, and he ate very little. He meditated for six years, twenty-four hours a day. And at the end of those six years he discovered something: he realized that people don't have to struggle so much. We don't have to give in so much to our hassles, our pain, our discomfort. The Buddha discovered that there is something in us known as basic goodness. Therefore, we don't have to condemn ourselves for being bad or naughty. The Buddha taught what he had learned to the

rest of mankind. What he taught then— twenty-five hundred years ago—is still being taught and practiced. The important point for us is to realize that we are basically good. Our only problem is that sometimes we don't actually acknowledge that goodness. We don't see it, so we blame somebody else or we blame ourselves. That is a mistake. We don't have to blame others, and we don't have to feel nasty or angry. Fundamental goodness is always with us, always in us.

CRAZY
MONKEY MIND

THE MIND is like a crazy monkey, which leaps about and never stays in one place. It is completely restless and constantly paranoid about its surroundings. The training, or the meditation practice, is a way to catch the monkey, to begin with. That is the starting point. Traditionally, this training is called *shamatha* in Sanskrit, or *shi-ne* in Tibetan, which means simply "the development of peace." When we talk about the development of peace, we are not talking about cultivating a peaceful state, as such, but about simplicity.

1 3

NO AMBITION

IN TRUE meditation, there is no ambition to stir up thoughts, nor is there an ambition to suppress them. They are just allowed to occur spontaneously and become an expression of basic sanity. They become the expression of the precision and the clarity of the awakened state of mind.

14

THE HEART OF
THE BUDDHA

HERE IS the really good news: We are intrinsically buddha, or intrinsically awake, and we are intrinsically good. Without exception, and without the need for analytical studies, we can say that we automatically have buddha within us. That is known as buddha-nature or *bodhichitta*, the heart of the Buddha.

15

GOING BEYOND FEAR

TRUE FEARLESSNESS is not the reduction of fear, but going beyond fear. Unfortunately, in the English language, we don't have one word that means that. Fearlessness is the closest term, but by fear*less* we don't mean "less fear," but "beyond fear." Going beyond fear begins when we examine our fear: our anxiety, nervousness, concern, and restlessness. If we look into our fear, if we look beneath its veneer, the first thing we find is sadness, beneath the nervousness. Nervousness is cranking up, vibrating, all the time. When we slow down, when we relax with our fear, we find sadness, which is calm and gentle. Sadness hits you in your heart, and your body produces a tear. Before you cry, there is a feeling in your chest and then, after that, you produce tears in your eyes. You are about to produce rain or a waterfall in your eyes, and you feel sad and lonely, and perhaps romantic at the same time. That is the first tip of fearlessness and the first sign of real warriorship. You might think that when you experience fearlessness you will hear the opening to Beethoven's Fifth Symphony or see a great explosion in the sky, but it doesn't happen that way. In the Shambhala tradition, discovering fearlessness comes from working with the softness of the human heart.

16

MAKE FRIENDS
WITH YOURSELF

WE GET angry with ourselves, saying, "I could do better than this. What's wrong with me? I seem to be getting worse. I'm going backward." We're angry at the whole world, including ourselves. Everything we see is an insult. The universe becomes the expression of total insult. One has to relate with that. If you are going to exert your power and energy to walk on the path, you have to work with yourself. The first step is to make friends with yourself. That is almost the motto of *shamatha* or mindfulness meditation experience. Making friends with yourself means accepting and acknowledging yourself. You work with your subconscious gossip, fantasies, dreams—everything. And everything that you learn about yourself you bring back to the technique, to the awareness of the breathing, which was taught by the Buddha.

AROUSE YOUR SENSE OF WAKEFULNESS

IN THE fundamental sense, Buddhist meditation does not involve meditating on anything. You simply arouse your sense of wakefulness and hold an excellent posture. You hold up your head and shoulders and sit cross-legged. Then very simply, you relate to the basic notion of body, speech, and mind, and you focus your awareness in some way, usually using the breath. You are breathing out and in, and you just experience that breathing very naturally. Your breath is not considered either holy or evil; it is just breath.

1 8

THE BOREDOM OF
MOUNTAINS AND
WATERFALLS

Boredom is important in meditation
practice; it increases the psychological
sophistication of the practitioners. They
begin to appreciate boredom and they develop their sophistication until the boredom begins to become cool boredom, like a
mountain river. It flows and flows and
flows, methodically and repetitiously, but it
is very cooling, very refreshing. Mountains
never get tired of being mountains, and waterfalls never get tired of being waterfalls.
Because of their patience we begin to appreciate them. There is something in that. If

we are to save ourselves from spiritual materialism and from *buddhadharma* with credentials, or dogma, if we are to become the dharma without credentials, the introduction of boredom and repetitiousness is extremely important.

THE TRUTH OF SUFFERING

WE MUST work with our fears, frustrations, disappointments, and irritations, the painful aspects of life. People complain that Buddhism is an extremely gloomy religion because it emphasizes suffering and misery. Usually religions speak of beauty, song, ecstasy, bliss. But according to Buddha, we must begin by seeing the experience of life as it is. We must see the truth of suffering, the reality of dissatisfaction. We cannot ignore it and attempt to examine only the glorious, pleasurable aspects of life. If one searches for a promised land, a Treasure Island, then the search only leads to more pain. So all sects and schools of Buddhism agree that we must begin by facing the reality of our living situations. We cannot begin by dreaming.

BASIC SANITY

IN CONTRAST to the traditional medical model of disturbances, the Buddhist approach is founded on the belief that basic sanity is operative in all states of mind. Confusion, from this point of view, is two-sided: it creates a need, a demand for sanity. This hungry nature of confusion is very powerful and very important. The demand for relief or sanity that is contained in confusion is, in fact, the beginning point of Buddhism. That is what moved Buddha to sit beneath the bodhi tree twenty-five hundred years ago—to confront his confusion and find its source—after struggling vainly for seven years in various ascetic yogic disciplines.

Basically, we are faced with a similar situation now in the West. Like Siddhartha before he became the Buddha, we are confused, anxious, and hungry psychologically. Despite a physically luxurious prosperity, there is a tremendous amount of emotional anxiety. This anxiety has stimulated a lot of research into various types of psychotherapy, drug therapy, behavior modification, and group therapies. From the Buddhist viewpoint, this search is evidence of the nature of basic sanity operating within neurosis.

BEING A PERSON
OF SANITY

I T IS through body, speech, and mind that
we relate with the phenomenal world.
Such a relationship is not necessarily spiritual; it is physical, bodily. It is a question of
being a person of sanity, a person of openness. In fact, we could almost approach the
whole path in a secular way and call it the
nontheistic discipline of developing sanity
and openness, rather than regarding it as
purely a religious tradition.

A GREAT FEAST

ONE OF the problems we have is that, in relating with the samsaric, confused emotions, we behave like misers; we are too frugal. We feel that we have something to lose and something to gain, so we work with the emotions just pinch by pinch. But when we work on the wisdom level, we think in terms of greater emotions: greater anger, greater passion, greater speed; therefore, we begin to lose our ground and our boundaries. Then we have nothing to fight for. Everything is our world, so what is the point of fighting? What is the point of segregating things in terms of this and that? The whole thing becomes a larger-scale affair, and ego's territory seems very cheap, almost inapplicable or nonexistent. That is why tantra is called a great feast.

23

A GLIMPSE OF
BUDDHA NATURE

A GLIMPSE of buddha nature is not a glimpse in the sense of viewing something: It is a gap rather than a glimpse. That gap is the experience that comes out of seeing through the veils of ego. But whether we have a glimpse of it or not, the buddha mind is still functioning in us all the time. It occurs in the most bizarre, cheap, and confused styles we might present, as well as in whatever extremely profound, dignified, and wise experiences we might have. All of those are the expressions of buddha nature.

24

BASIC GOODNESS

EVERYBODY POSSESSES the uncondi-
tioned possibility of cheerfulness, which
is not connected purely with either pain or
pleasure. You have an inclination: In the
flash of one second, you feel what needs to
be done. It is not a product of your education; it is not scientific or logical; you simply pick up on the message. And then you
act: You just do it. That basic human quality of suddenly opening up is the best part
of human instinct. You know what to do
right away, on the spot—which is fantastic.
That is what we call the dot of basic goodness and unconditional instinct. You don't
think: You just feel, on the spot. Basic trust

is knowing that there is such a thing as that spark of basic goodness. Although you might be in the worst of the worst shape, still that goodness does exist.

25

THE GOLDEN CHAIN
OF SPIRITUALITY

As LONG as we follow a spiritual approach promising salvation, miracles, liberation, then we are bound by the "golden chain of spirituality." Such a chain might be beautiful to wear, with its inlaid jewels and intricate carvings, but nevertheless, it imprisons us. People think they can wear the golden chain for decoration without being imprisoned by it, but they are deceiving themselves. As long as one's approach to spirituality is based upon enriching ego, then it is spiritual materialism, a suicidal process rather than a creative one.

26

SECULAR
ENLIGHTENMENT

IN TIBET, as well as many other Asian
countries, there are stories about a leg-
endary kingdom that was a place of peace
and prosperity, governed by wise and compassionate rulers. The citizens were equally
kind and learned, so that, in general, the
kingdom was a model society. This place
was called Shambhala. Among many Tibetan
Buddhist teachers, there has long been a tradition that regards the kingdom of Shambhala not as an external place but as the
ground or root of wakefulness and sanity
that exists as a potential within every human being. From that point of view, it is

not important to decide whether the kingdom of Shambhala is fact or fiction. Instead, we should appreciate and emulate the ideal of an enlightened society that it represents. The Shambhala teachings use the image of the Shambhala kingdom to represent the ideal of secular enlightenment, that is, the possibility of uplifting our personal existence and that of others without the need for any religious outlook. With the great problems now facing human society, it seems increasingly important to find simple and nonsectarian ways to work with ourselves and to share our understanding with others.

27

LEAP OF DARING

IN ORDER to overcome selfishness, it is necessary to be daring. It is as though you were dressed in your swimsuit, standing on the diving board with a pool in front of you, and you asked yourself: "Now what?" The obvious answer is: "Jump." That is daring. You might wonder if you will sink or hurt yourself if you jump. You might. There is no insurance, but it is worthwhile jumping to find out what will happen. The student warrior has to jump. We are so accustomed to accepting what is bad for us and rejecting what is good for us. We are attracted to our cocoons, our selfishness, and we are afraid of selflessness, stepping beyond ourselves. So in order to overcome our hesitation about giving up our privacy, and in order to commit ourselves to others' welfare, some kind of leap is necessary.

28

THE FUTURE IS IN
OUR HANDS

WE HOLD the threshold of the future of the world in our hands, on our path. When we say this, we are not dreaming. We are not exaggerating. We hold a tremendous hope, maybe the only hope for the future dark age.

We have a lot of responsibilities, and those responsibilities are not easy to fulfill. They won't come along easily, like an ordinary success story. They have to be stitched, painted, carved, step by step, inch by inch, minute by minute. It will be manual work. There will be no automatic big sweep, or solution.

When something good is done in the world, it is usually difficult. It is manual, rather than automatic. When something bad is done, usually that is automatic. Evil things are easy to catch, but good ones are dicult to catch. They go against the grain of ordinary habitual tendencies.

29

DEVELOPING
FEARLESS
RENUNCIATION

THE GROUND of fearlessness and the basis of overcoming doubt and wrong belief is to develop renunciation. Renunciation here means overcoming that very hard, tough, aggressive mentality that wards off any gentleness that might come into our hearts. Fear does not allow fundamental tenderness to enter into us. When tenderness tinged by sadness touches our heart, we know that we are in contact with reality. We feel it. That contact is genuine, fresh, and quite raw. That sensitivity is the basic experience of warriorship, and it is the key to developing fearless renunciation.

30

ACCEPTING
IMPERFECTIONS

W E MUST be willing to be completely ordinary people, which means accepting ourselves as we are without trying to become greater, purer, more spiritual, more insightful. If we can accept our imperfections as they are, quite ordinarily, then we can use them as part of the path. But if we try to get rid of our imperfections, then they will be enemies, obstacles on the road to our "self-improvement." And the same is true for the breath in meditation. If we can see it as it is, without trying to use it to improve ourselves, then it becomes a part of the path because we are no longer using it as the tool of our personal ambition.

ETERNALLY RICH

THE BASIC practice of richness is learning to project the goodness that exists in your being, so that a sense of goodness shines out. When you feel that your life is established properly and fully, you feel that a golden rain is continuously descending. It feels solid, simple, and straightforward. Then you also have a feeling of gentleness and openness, as though an exquisite flower has bloomed auspiciously in your life. Although at that particular point you might be penniless, there is no problem. You are suddenly, eternally rich.

GLIMPSE OF
ENLIGHTENMENT

FUNDAMENTALLY the idea of enlightenment—the notion or term "enlightenment" or "buddha" or "awakened one"—implies tremendous sharpness and precision along with a sense of spaciousness. We can experience this; it is not myth at all. We experience a glimpse of it, and the point is to start from that glimpse and gradually, as you become more familiar with that glimpse and the possibilities of reigniting it, it happens naturally. There occurs a flash, maybe a fraction of a second. These flashes happen constantly, all the time. Faith is realizing that there is some open space and sharpness in your everyday life.

3 3

A NATURAL STATE
OF AWARENESS

AWARENESS DOES not mean be careful, ward off danger, you might step into a puddle, so beware. That is not the kind of awareness we are talking about. We are talking about unconditional presence, which is not expected to be there all the time. In fact, in order to be completely aware, you have to disown the experience of awareness. It cannot be regarded as yours—it is just there and you do not try to hold on to it. Then, somehow, a general clarity takes place. So awareness is a glimpse rather than a continuous state. If you hold on to awareness, it becomes self-consciousness rather than awareness. Awareness has to be unmanufactured; it has to be a natural state.

34

SPIRITUALITY
WITHOUT
MATERIALISM

IN THE spiritual materialistic approach, spirituality is regarded as bringing happiness. You say to yourself, "I could take off into the mountains and meditate in a cave. It will be a much simpler and more pleasurable life. I won't be bound by any obligations to anything at all. I won't have to answer the telephone. I won't have to maintain my house. I'll enjoy the fresh air. Meditation will come naturally, once there are no disturbances. There will be no one to irritate me, because I've abandoned those dirty associations from my past history. I won't care who I was, but I will care who I *am,* living in the mountains, enjoying the beauty of nature, the fresh air, and vibrations." However, something is uncertain or missing from this whole vision.

It has been said that compassion is important, as well as wisdom. Spirituality without spiritual materialism is an attitude of compassion. Finally, you have to return to the world. And not just finally, but you have to work with the world. You have to relate with the world, because enlightened mind contains both wisdom as well as compassion simultaneously. So you have an obligation to the world that brought you up, the world that you belong to.

35

DISAPPOINTMENT

WE MIGHT think that in the spiritual search we are simply concerned with fulfillment, happiness, accomplishment, and enlightenment. But at the same time the spiritual path requires some sacrifice, some act of generosity, some kind of training before we reach happiness and goodness. Therefore, the idea of disappointment plays an important role. In this case "disappointment" means we cannot fulfill every expectation of ego, nor can we achieve everything that we want to achieve without any giving or any openness. In other words, disappointment means that we cannot become self-made buddhas. We have to experience the reality of life as such before we can decide to proclaim ourselves to be enlightened.

36

UNCONDITIONAL
CHEERFULNESS

TRANSPLANTING THE moon of wakefulness into your heart and the sun of wisdom into your head can be natural and obvious. It is not so much trying to look for the bright side of life and using that side of things as a stepping-stone, but it is discovering unconditional cheerfulness, which has no other side. It is just one side, one taste. From that, the natural sense of goodness begins to dawn in your heart. Therefore, whatever we experience, whatever we see, whatever we hear, whatever we think—all those activities begin to have some sense of holiness or sacredness in them. The world is full of hospitality at that point. Sharp corners begin to dissolve and the darkness begins to be uplifted in our lives. That kind of goodness is unconditionally good, and at that point, we become a decent human being and a warrior. Such an approach has to be accompanied by the sitting practice of meditation. The practice of meditation acts as a training ground and stronghold. Out of that, the seed of friendliness begins to occur. The main point is to appreciate your world. That kind of world is known as the *vajra,* or indestructible, world. It is a cheerful world. It never becomes too good or too bad.

37

NONEXISTENCE

NONEXISTENCE IS the only preparation for tantra, the highest teachings of Buddhism, and we should realize that there is no substitute. The experience of nonexistence brings a sense of delightful humor and, at the same time, complete openness and freedom. In addition, it brings an experience of complete indestructibility that is unchallengeable, immovable, and completely solid. The experience of indestructibility can only occur when we realize that nonexistence is possible, in the sense of being without reference points, without philosophical definitions, without even the notion of nonexistence.

38

TRANSCENDING
KARMA

OUR PRESENT state of mind, our present spiritual development, or present domestic situation has been karmically determined up to this point by life situations in the past. The birth of further karma occurs through the constant reliving of the past. We reproduce the nest or ground or home, so that we can function continuously. Therefore, the practice of meditation is the only path that can work with karma as such.

Karma in this case is the psychological aspect of the continuity of impulse, emotions, and the subconscious mental processes that go on. These processes feed on themselves all the time, developing further, constantly, on and on. So unless there is a way of not feeding the subconscious mind, there is no way of preventing karmic situations. It doesn't matter whether we are dealing with good karma or bad karma. Both of those are the same kind of situations, from this point of view. Even if we are sowing seeds of good karma, we are nevertheless still encircled in a samsaric fortress. So from this point of view, meditation practice is a way of stepping out of that karmic situation altogether—transcending both good and bad.

39

CRAZY WISDOM

USING THE word *crazy* from the English language to describe tantric experience is very tricky because of the various ideas we have about craziness. Being crazy is associated with the idea of being absurd, on the edge of lunacy. There is also a notion of craziness as being unconventional. And sometimes we talk about somebody being crazy about music or crazy about honey or sugar. I don't think crazy wisdom fits any of these examples. Instead, crazy wisdom is the basic norm or the basic logic of sanity. It is a transparent view that cuts through conventional norms or conventional emotionalism. It is the notion of relating properly with the world. It is knowing how much heat is needed to boil water to make a cup of tea, or how much pressure you should apply to educate your students. That level of craziness is very wise.

Such a wise person is well-versed in the ways of the world, and he or she has developed and understood basic logic. He knows how to build a campfire, how to pitch a tent, and how to brush his teeth. He knows how to handle himself in relating with the world, from the level of knowing how to make a good fire in the fireplace up to knowing the fine points of philosophy. So there is absolute knowledgeability. And then, on top of that, craziness begins to descend, as an ornament to the basic wisdom that is already there.

40

THREE TYPES OF
GENEROSITY

TRADITIONALLY, there are three types of generosity. The first one is ordinary generosity, giving material goods or providing comfortable situations for others. The second one is the gift of fearlessness. You reassure others and teach them that they don't have to feel completely tormented and freaked out about their existence. You help them to see that there is basic goodness and spiritual practice, that there is a way for them to sustain their lives. The third type of generosity is the gift of dharma, the teachings. You show others that there is a path that consists of discipline, meditation, and intellect or knowledge. Through all three types of generosity, you can open other people's minds. In that way their closedness, wretchedness, and small thinking can be turned into a larger vision.

NO ENEMY

FOR THE Shambhala warrior, the actual, basic notion of victory is not so much that you have one-upped your enemy and therefore you are victorious. Rather, no enemy exists at all; therefore, there is victory. This is the idea of unconditional warriorship and unconditional victory. In connection with this, the concept of sacredness is that fearlessness is carried into everyday life situations, even brushing your teeth. So fearlessness occurs all over the place, all the time. Fearlessness here is also unconditional. In this way, fearlessness becomes cheerful and very light. There's no need for cowardice or fear at all, or any moments of doubt. Actually what we're talking about is doubtlessness, we could say, rather than fearlessness. There's no doubt. There are no second thoughts. Everything is a complete warrior's world. So here victory is not having to deal with an enemy at all. It is the notion of no enemy. The whole world is a friend.

EMPTINESS

WHEN WE talk of emptiness, it means
the absence of solidity, the absence
of fixed notions which cannot be changed,
which have no relationship to us at all but
which remain as they are, separate. The solidity of experience is a certain kind of de-
termination not to give away, not to open.
We would like to keep everything intact
purely for the purpose of security, of
knowing where we are. You are afraid to
change. That sort of solidness is form. In
the Buddha's teachings on emptiness, the
statement "form is empty" refers to the absence of that security; you see everything
as penetrating and open. But that doesn't
mean that everything has to be completely

formless, or nothing. When we talk of nothingness, emptiness, or voidness, we are not talking in terms of negatives but in terms of nothingness being everything. It's another way of saying "everything"—but it is much safer to say "nothing" at that particular level than "everything."

43

THE SOFT SPOT OF
COMPASSION

COMPASSION IS based on some sense of
"soft spot" in us. It is as if we had a
pimple on our body that was very sore— so
sore that we do not want to rub it or
scratch it. That sore spot on our body is
an analogy for compassion. Why? Because
even in the midst of immense aggression,
insensitivity to our life, or laziness, we always have a soft spot, some point we can
cultivate—or at least not bruise. Every human being has that kind of basic sore spot,
including animals. Whether we are crazy,
dull, aggressive, ego-tripping, whatever we
might be, there is still that sore spot taking

place in us. An open wound, which might be a more vivid analogy, is always there. We are not completely covered with a suit of armor all the time. We have a sore spot somewhere, some open wound somewhere. Such a relief! Thank earth!

44

IDIOT COMPASSION

IDIOT COMPASSION is the highly conceptualized idea that you want to do good. Of course, according to the mahayana teachings of Buddhism you should do everything for everybody; there is no selection involved at all. But that doesn't mean to say that you have to be gentle all the time. Your gentleness should have heart, strength. In order that your compassion doesn't become idiot compassion, you have to use your intelligence. Otherwise, there could be self-indulgence, thinking that you are creating a compassionate situation when in fact you are feeding the other person's aggression. If you go to a shop and the shopkeeper cheats you and you go back and let him cheat you again, that doesn't seem to be a very healthy thing to do for others.

45

THE WIND OF AWARENESS

IN TALKING about open mind, we are re-ferring to a kind of openness that is re-lated with letting self-existing awareness come to us. Awareness is not something that needs to be manufactured: When there is a gap, awareness enters into us. So aware-ness does not require a certain particular effort. Awareness is like a wind. If you open your doors and windows, it is bound to come in.

46

WINDHORSE

THERE IS an uplifted quality that exists in our lives. You could call it sacred existence, which is automatically created because of your mindfulness and awareness. We pay attention to details: we wash the dishes, we clean our room, we press our shirts, and we fold the sheets. When we pay attention to everything around us, the overall effect is upliftedness. The Shambhalian term for that is *windhorse*. The wind principle is very airy and powerful. Horse means that the energy is rideable. That particular airy and sophisticated energy, so clean and full of decency, can be ridden. You don't just have a bird flying by itself in the sky, but you have something to ride on. Such energy is fresh and exuberant but, at the same time, rideable. Therefore, it is known as windhorse.

47

LOOK!

Look. This is your world! You can't not look. There is no other world. This is your world; it is your feast. You inherited this; you inherited these eyeballs; you inherited this world of color. Look at the greatness of the whole thing. Look! don't hesitate—look! open your eyes. don't blink, and look, look—look further.

Then you might *see* something. The more you look, the more inquisitive you are, the more you are bound to see. Your looking process is not restrained, because you are genuine, you are gentle, you have nothing to lose, and you have nothing to fight against. You can look so much, you can look further, and then you can see so beautifully. In fact, you can feel the warmth of red and the coolness of blue and the richness of yellow and the penetrating quality of green—all at once. You appreciate the world around you. It is a fantastic new discovery of the world.

48

ELEGANCE

ELEGANCE MEANS appreciating things as they are. There is a sense of delight and of fearlessness. You are not fearful of dark corners. If there are any dark, mysterious corners, black and confusing, you override them with your glory, sense of beauty, your sense of cleanness, your feeling of being regal. Because you can override fearfulness in this way, tantra, or the highest stage in Tibetan Buddhist practice, is known as the king of all the *yanas* or stages on the path. You take an attitude of having perfectly complete and very rich basic sanity.

49

ILLUMINATION

ENLIGHTENMENT IS referred to as en-*lighten*-ment, rather than as a big gain of freedom. It is further luminosity: it illuminates life. Up to this point, we had a very bad lighting system; but now we are getting a better lighting system, so we begin to see every curve of skin, every inch of our world, properly. We might get very irritated by such sharpness and precision, but that seems to be part of the perspective.

50

BEING KIND
TO YOURSELF

WE HAVE to learn to be kinder to ourselves, much more kind. Smile a lot, although nobody is watching you smile. Listen to your own brook, echoing yourself. You can do a good job. In the sitting practice of meditation, when you begin to be still, hundreds of thousands, millions, and billions of thoughts will go through your mind. But they just pass through, and only the worthy ones leave their fish eggs behind. We have to leave ourselves some time to be. You're not going to see the Shambhala vision, you're not even going to survive unless you leave yourself a minute to be, a minute to smile. Please give yourself a good time.

51

JUST BE

JUST BE with your breath; be with your discursive thoughts. That purity brings a sense of relief and a sense of peace, which is known as individual salvation. Peace in this case means being without complications. It is not a state of tranquility per se; it is just basic simplicity and basic ordinariness. That peace, that simplicity, is empty by nature. It has nothing to dwell on or with; therefore, it is basically fresh and clean and free from dirt, free from sloppiness. It is empty.

A SUBTLE TWIST
OF MIND

LITTLE THINGS cause a shift in our attention, no matter how small or little they
might be. But in the end, things tend to
get exaggerated immensely. So suffering
comes from such little twists that take place
in our life. That first little hint of dislike for
somebody or that first hint of attraction for
somebody eventually escalates and could
bring on a much more immense scale of
emotional drama or psychodrama. Everything starts from a minute scale at the
beginning and then expands. It begins to
swell, so to speak, and expand in that way
until it becomes very large—immeasurably

large in a lot of cases. We experience our-selves that way. Within that frame of refer-ence, that subtle shift of attention seems to be the important cause of suffering in our life. Such shifts of attention make emotions as they are: aggression, passion, ignorance, and all the rest of them. They are seemingly very heavy-handed and large-scale and crude. But they have their origin in a sub-tle twist that takes place in our mind con-stantly, all the time.

53

DROP ALL
REFERENCE POINTS

WE MUST drop all reference points, all concepts of what is or what should be. Then it is possible to experience the uniqueness and vividness of phenomena directly. There is tremendous room to experience things, to allow experience to occur and pass away. Movement happens within vast space. Whatever happens, pleasure and pain, birth and death, and so forth, are not interfered with but are experienced in their fullest flavor. Whether they are sweet or sour, they are experienced completely, without philosophical overlays or emotional attitudes to make things seem lovable or presentable. We are never trapped in life, because there are constant opportunities for creativity, challenges for improvisation. Ironically, by seeing clearly and acknowledging our egolessness, we may discover that suffering contains bliss, impermanence contains continuity or eternity, and egolessness contains the earth quality of solid being. But this transcendental bliss, continuity, and beingness are not based on fantasies, ideas, or fears.

54

ONE TRUTH

THE ESSENCE of samsara, or confused existence, is found in the misunderstandings of bewilderment, passion, and aggression. Unless you relate to these as path—understanding them, working with them, treading on them—you do not discover the goal. So therefore, as Buddha says, "Suffering should be realized, the origin should be overcome and, by that, cessation should be realized because the path should be seen as the truth." Seeing the truth as it is, is the goal as well as the path. For that matter, discovering the truth of samsara is the discovery of nirvana, liberation, for truth does not depend on other formulas or alternative answers. The reality of samsara is equally the reality of nirvana. This truth is seen as one truth without relativity.

55

TRUTH IS LIKE
A THUNDERBOLT

*D*HARMA LITERALLY means "truth" or "norm." It is a particular way of thinking, a way of viewing the world, which is not a concept but experience. This particular truth is very painful truth—usually truths are. It rings with the sound of reality, which comes too close to home. We become completely embarrassed when we begin to hear the truth. It is wrong to think that the truth is going to sound fantastic and beautiful, like a flute solo. The truth is actually like a thunderbolt. It wakes you up and makes you think twice whether you should stay in the rain or move into the house. Provocative.

56

THE GREAT JOY

MEDITATION PRACTICE is based on dropping dualistic fixation, dropping the struggle of good against bad. There are many references in the tantric literature to *mahasukha,* the great joy, but the reason it is referred to as the great joy is because it transcends both hope and fear, pain and pleasure. Joy here is not pleasurable in the ordinary sense, but it is an ultimate and fundamental sense of freedom, a sense of humor, the ability to see the ironical aspect of the game of ego, the play of polarities. If one is able to see ego from an aerial point of view, then one is able to see its humorous quality.

57

SEEING THE
TRANSPARENCY
OF CONCEPTS

IN THE absence of thoughts and emotions, the lords, or the forces, of materialism bring up a still more powerful weapon, concepts. Labeling phenomena creates a feeling of a solid, definite world of "things." Such a solid world reassures us that we are a solid, continuous thing as well. The world exists, therefore I, the perceiver of the world, exist. Meditation involves seeing the transparency of concepts, so that labeling no longer serves as a way of solidifying our world and our image of self. Labeling becomes simply the act of discrimination.

58

PURIFICATION

PURIFICATION IS learning to relate with problems. Does a problem exist or not? Is the problem a problem, or is the problem a promise? We are not talking about how to get rid of problems or impurities here, as though we were suddenly surrounded by piles of garbage that we want to clean up. That is not the point. The point is to discover the quality of garbageness. Before we dispose of our garbage, first we have to examine it. If we approached purification as simply trying to get rid of our garbage, we would do a great job of emitting spiritual pollution into the atmosphere.

59

THE ABSENCE
OF STRUGGLE
IS FREEDOM

BY THE examination of his own thoughts, emotions, concepts, and the other activities of mind, the Buddha discovered that there is no need to struggle to prove our existence, that we need not be subject to the rule of the lords or forces of materialism. There is no need to struggle to be free; the absence of struggle is in itself freedom. This egoless state is the attainment of buddhahood. The process of transforming the material of mind from expressions of ego's ambition into expressions of basic sanity and enlightenment through the practice of meditation—this might be said to be the true spiritual path.

60

REAL HUMILITY

Humility, very simply, is the absence of arrogance. Where there is no arrogance, you relate with your world as an eye-level situation, without one-upmanship. Because of that, there can be a genuine interchange. Nobody is using their message to put anybody else down, and nobody has to come down or up to the other person's level. Everything is eye-level. Humility in the Shambhala tradition also involves some kind of playfulness, which is a sense of humor. In most religious traditions, you feel humble because of a fear of punishment, pain, and sin. In the Shambhala world you feel full of it. You feel healthy and good. In fact, you feel proud. Therefore, you feel

humility. That's one of the Shambhala contradictions or, we could say, dichotomies.
Real humility is genuineness.

6 1

THE WARRIOR IS NOT AFRAID OF SPACE

THE COWARD lives in constant terror of space: Afraid of darkness because he can't see anything, afraid of silence because he can't hear anything. The setting-sun world teaches you to wear a suit of armor to protect yourself. But what are you protecting yourself from? Space. The challenge of warriorship is to step out of the cocoon, to step out into space, by being brave and at the same time gentle.

6 2

BRAVERY
INVOKES MAGIC

THE BEST and only way to invoke *drala*, or magic, is by creating an atmosphere of bravery. The fundamental aspect of bravery is *being without deception*. Deception in this case is self-deception, doubting yourself. Usually if we say someone is brave, we mean that he is not afraid of any enemy or he is willing to die for a cause or he is never intimidated. The Shambhala understanding of bravery is quite different. Here bravery is the courage to be—to live in the world without any deception and with tremendous kindness and caring for others. You might wonder how this can bring magic into your life. The ordinary idea of magic is that you can conquer the elements, so that you can turn earth into fire or fire into water or ignore the law of gravity and fly. But true magic is the magic of *reality,* as it is: The earth of earth, the water of water—communicating with the elements so that, in some sense, they become one with you. When you develop bravery, you make a connection with the elemental quality of existence. Bravery begins to heighten your existence, that is, to bring out the brilliant and genuine qualities of your environment and of your being.

63

LET THINGS TAKE
THEIR COURSE

IN THE practice of meditation, when
bodily pain or pleasure arises, just perceive it and just leave it. You do not have to
put it through any process of any kind.
Each situation is unique. Therefore you just
go along with it, let it happen according to
its nature. It is a matter of acceptance. Even
though the acceptance of what is happening
may be confusing, just accept the given situation and do not try to make it something
else; do not try to make it into an educa-
tional process at all. Just see it, perceive it,
and then abandon it.

If you experience something and then disown that experience, you provide a space between that knowledge and yourself, which permits it simply to take its course. Disowning is like the yeast in the fermentation process. That process brews a state of mind in which you begin to learn and feel properly.

64

THE NONVIOLENT APPROACH

To develop *ahimsa*, or the nonviolent approach, first of all you have to see that your problems are not really trying to destroy you. Usually, we immediately try to get rid of our problems. We think that there are forces operating against us and that we have to get rid of them. The important thing is to learn to be friendly toward our problems, by developing what is called *metta* in Pali, *maitri* in Sanskrit, or loving-kindness in English.

65

PROBLEMS AS OPPORTUNITIES

THE ATTITUDE that results from the Buddhist orientation and practice is quite different from the "mistake mentality." One actually experiences mind as fundamentally pure, that is, healthy and positive, and "problems" as temporary and superficial defilements. Such a viewpoint does not quite mean getting rid of problems, but rather shifting one's focus. Problems are seen in a much broader context of health: one begins to let go of clinging to one's neuroses and to step beyond obsession and identification with them. The emphasis is no longer on the problems themselves but rather on the ground of experience through realizing the nature of mind itself. When problems are seen in this way, then there is less panic and everything seems more workable. When problems arise, instead of being seen as purely threats, they become learning situations, opportunities to find out more about one's own mind, and to continue on one's journey.

66

TELL THE TRUTH

TRUTH ALWAYS works. There always has to be basic honesty; that is the source of trust. When someone sees that you are telling the truth, then they will realize further that you are saying something worthwhile and trustworthy. It always works.

There are no special tips on how to trick people into sanity by not telling the truth. I don't think there can be such a thing at all. At least I haven't found it in dealing with my own students. Sometimes telling the truth is very painful to them, but they begin to realize it is the truth, and they appreciate it sooner or later.

It is also important to realize that you

don't have to have control over others. You see, that is exactly the truth situation: You do not have all the answers; you are not assuming control over people. Instead, you are trying to tell the truth—in the beginning, in the middle, and at the end.

THE BIG NO

THERE IS no special reality beyond reality. That is the Big no, as opposed to the regular no. You *cannot* destroy life. You cannot by any means, for any religious, spiritual, or metaphysical reasons, step on an ant or kill your mosquitoes—at all. That is Buddhism. That is Shambhala. You have to respect *everybody*. You cannot make a random judgment on that at all. That is the rule of the kingdom of Shambhala, and that is the Big no. You can't act on your desires alone. You have to contemplate the details of what needs to be removed and what needs to be cultivated.

AWAKENING CONFIDENCE

WARRIORSHIP REFERS to realizing the power, dignity, and wakefulness that are inherent in all of us as human beings. It is awakening our basic human confidence, which allows us to cheer up, develop a sense of vision, and succeed in what we are doing. Because warriorship is innate in human beings, the way to become a warrior—or the warrior's path—is to see who and what we are as human beings and cultivate that. If we look at ourselves directly, without hesitation or embarrassment, we find that we have a lot of strength and a lot of resources available constantly.

THE COSMIC WOUND

ALTHOUGH WE may feel as though we're covered with a cast-iron shield, a sore spot always exists in us, which is fantastic. That sore spot is known as embryonic compassion, potential compassion. At least we have some kind of gap, some discrepancy in our state of being, which allows basic sanity to shine through. Not only that, but there is also an inner wound, which is called *tatha-gatagarbha,* or buddha nature. Buddha nature is like a heart that is sliced and bruised by wisdom and compassion. When the external wound and the internal wound begin to meet and to communicate, then we begin to realize that our whole being is made out of one complete sore spot altogether. That vulnerability is compassion. We really have no way to defend ourselves anymore at all. A gigantic cosmic wound is all over the place—an inward wound and an external wound at the same time. Both are sensitive to cold air, hot air, and little disturbances of atmosphere which begin to affect us both inwardly and outwardly. It is the living flame of love, if you would like to call it that.

70

DISCONTINUITY

THERE'S A sense of impermanence that happens constantly, all the time. That's the starting point, to realize that you can't hang on to one continuous continuation, that things *do* change constantly, and that you have no permanent security. There's only one eternity, and that's the eternity of discontinuity.

UNCONDITIONAL FREEDOM

FREEDOM—unexpected, undemanded freedom. Freedom cannot be bought or bartered for. Freedom doesn't come cheap or expensive. It just happens. It is only without any reference point that freedom can evolve. That is why it is known as freedom—because it is unconditional. So it is our duty—in fact, we might even go as far as to say it is the purpose of our life—it is our heroic duty to encourage the notion of freedom as it is, without contamination by any further pollution of this and that and that and this. No bargaining.

We have to maintain ourselves in an erect posture in order to work with freedom. The practice of meditation in the Buddhist tradition is extremely simple, extremely erect, and direct. There is a sense of pride in the fact that you are going to sit and practice meditation. When you sit and practice meditation, you don't do anything at all. You just sit and work with your breathing, your posture. You just sit and let all these thoughts come alive. You let your hidden neurosis come through. Let the discipline evolve itself.

ONE THING
AT A TIME

TWO THINGS cannot happen at once; it is impossible. It is easy to imagine that two things are happening at once, because our journey back and forth between the two may be very speedy. But even then we are doing only one thing at a time. The idea of mindfulness of mind is to slow down the fickleness of jumping back and forth. We have to realize that we are not extraordinary mental acrobats. We are not all that well trained. And even an extraordinarily well-trained mind could not manage that many things at once—not even two. But because things are very simple and direct, we can focus on, be aware and mindful of, one thing at a time. That one-pointedness, that bare attention, seems to be the basic point.

73

ONE STONE
KILLS ONE BIRD

SET ASIDE a time for sitting practice that is especially allocated for that practice. Don't say to yourself, "Well, I'm going to visit my girlfriend and I have to drive, so on my way to my girlfriend's I'll use driving as my meditation." That approach to mindfulness becomes too utilitarian, too pragmatic—killing two birds with one stone. "That way I meditate and I get a chance to see my girlfriend at the end, too." But something has to be given up somewhere. Some renunciation somewhere is necessary. One stone kills one bird.

74

EARTH IS MY WITNESS

A T THE dawn of his enlightenment, someone asked the Buddha, "What are your credentials? How do we know that you are enlightened?" He touched his hand to the ground. "This solid earth is my witness. This solid earth, this sane earth, is my witness." Sane and solid and definite, no imaginings, no concepts, no emotions, no frivolity, but being basically what is: this is the awakened state. And this is the example we follow in our meditation practice.

75

OPEN YOUR MIND

THE MORE you learn about your own mind, the more you learn about other people's minds. You begin to appreciate other worlds, other people's life situations. You are learning to extend your vision beyond what is just there in your immediate situation, on the spot, so your mind is opened that much more. And that reflects on your work with others. It makes you more skillful in deeds and also gives you more of a sense of warmth and compassion, so you become more accommodating of others.

76

SWITCHING OUR
ALLEGIANCE

BECOMING A warrior means that we can look directly at ourselves, see the nature of our cowardly mind, and step out of it. We can trade our small-minded struggle for security for a much vaster vision, one of fearlessness, openness, and genuine heroism. This doesn't happen all at once but is a gradual process. Our first inkling of that possibility comes when we begin to sense the claustrophobia and stuffiness of our self-imposed cocoon. At that point, our safe home begins to feel like a trap and we begin to sense that an alternative is possible. We begin to have tremendous longing for some kind of ventilation, and finally we actually experience a delightful breath of fresh air coming into our stale nest. At this point, we realize that it has been our choice all along to live in this restrictive, and by now somewhat revolting, mentality of defensiveness and cowardice. Simultaneously, we realize that we could just as easily switch our allegiance. We could break out of our dark, stuffy prison into the fresh air where it is possible for us to stretch our legs, to walk, run, or even dance and play. We realize that we could drop the oppressive struggle it takes to maintain our cowardice, and relax instead in the greater space of confidence.

77

SACREDNESS VERSUS SUPERSTITION

THERE IS a great deal of difference between sacredness and superstition. Superstition is believing something that you've been told, such as that if somebody drops a rotten egg on your head, it is bad luck. Superstition has no foundation in basic practice. Sacredness, however, is like the experience when you look at pure gold: you get some transmission of pure goldness because gold is pure and good. Similarly, when you converse with a person of great wisdom, the conversation doesn't necessarily have to be profound per se—it could just be "hello" and "good-bye"—but you experience the basic nature of goodness coming out of that person. Sacredness is like putting on a fur coat in the biting cold of winter. Sacredness fulfills its purposes, and it also brings cheerfulness and goodness into our system so that we don't pollute the world. Sacredness is what allows us to say that the Shambhala principles can create an enlightened society.

78

THE ENVIRONMENT
AROUND THE BREATH

As far as Buddha was concerned, at the point of his enlightenment, it was not the message but the implications that were more important. And as followers of Buddha, we have this approach, which is the idea of *vipashyana,* literally meaning "insight." Insight is relating not only with what you see but also with the implications of it, the totality of the space and objects around it. Breath is the object of meditation, but the environment around the breath is also part of the meditative situation.

79

A TRADITION
OF OPENNESS

TAKING THE *bodhisattva* vow to help others implies that instead of holding our own individual territory and defending it tooth and nail, we become open to the world that we are living in. It means we are willing to take on greater responsibility, immense responsibility. In fact, it means taking a big chance. But taking such a chance is not false heroism or personal eccentricity. It is a chance that has been taken in the past by millions of bodhisattvas, enlightened ones, and great teachers. So a tradition of responsibility and openness has been handed down from generation to generation, and now we too are participating in the sanity and dignity of this tradition.

FEARLESS NO

FEARLESSNESS IS extending ourselves beyond a limited view. In the *Heart Sutra,* one of the Buddha's essential teachings, it talks about going beyond. Gone beyond, or *ga-te* in Sanskrit, is the basic no. In the sutra, it says there is no eye, no ear, no sound, no smell—all of those things. When you experience egolessness, the solidity of your life and your perceptions falls apart. That could be very desolate or it could be very inspiring, in terms of *shunyata,* or the Buddhist understanding of emptiness. Very simply, it is basic no. It is a real expression of fearlessness. In the Buddhist view, egolessness is preexisting, beyond our preconceptions. In the state of egolessness everything is simple and very clear. When we try to supplement the brightness of ego-lessness by putting a lot of other things onto it, those things obscure its brilliance, be-coming blockages and veils.

NOT REJECTING
OUR WORLD

WITHOUT THIS world, we cannot attain enlightenment. Without this
world, there would be no journey. By rejecting the world we would be rejecting
the ground and rejecting the path. All our
past history and all our neuroses are related
with others in some sense. All our experiences are based on others, basically. As long
as we have a sense of practice, some realization that we are treading on the path,
every one of those little details, which are
seemingly obstacles to us, becomes an essential part of the path. Without them, we
cannot attain anything at all—we have no

feedback, we have nothing to work with, absolutely nothing to work with. So in a sense all the things taking place around our world, all the irritations and all the problems, are crucial.

CONFUSION IS OUR
WORKING BASIS

A STUDENT once asked me, "How do you deal with confusion? How do you use it?" Well, what else do you have? The point is that we should find some working basis as soon as possible. Confusion is the first ordinary thing; it's how to begin. I think it's very important and absolutely necessary for everyone to know that we should find a stepping-stone rather than looking for an ideal situation. People may say, "When I retire from my job, I'll build my house on a beautiful coast, plant my garden, organize my house, and *then* I'm really going to sit and meditate!" That is not quite the way to go about it. We have to do something right away.

83

SUPERHUMAN
INSTINCT

THE USUAL human instinct is to feed ourselves first and only make friends with others if they can feed us. This could be called "ape instinct." But in the case of the *bodhisattva* vow, when we agree to put others first, we are talking about a kind of superhuman instinct that is much deeper and more full than that. Inspired by this instinct, we are willing to feel empty and deprived and confused. But something comes out of our willingness to feel that way, which is that we can help somebody else at the same time. So there is room for our confusion and chaos and ego-centeredness: They become stepping-stones. Even the irritations that occur in the practice of the bodhisattva path become a way of confirming our commitment.

84

SOMEBODY
BECAME BUDDHA

IT'S VERY moving to know that somebody
in the past became Buddha. Two thousand five hundred years ago a guy called
Siddhartha became Buddha. He actually did
those things and made an enormous impact
and impression on people—so enormous
that we still continue to follow his way and
share his ideas. It's very powerful that
somebody actually achieved enlightenment
and went so far as to proclaim it, and to
teach, and to share his life of eighty years
with his students. He spoke; he taught; and
he showed us how to behave, how to handle
ourselves with other people. It's an ex-

tremely powerful experience. Enlightenment is no longer a myth or concept, but something that actually did take place. It did happen—I think that is the basis of our conviction.

QUESTIONING

BUDDHA NATURE is not regarded as a peaceful state of mind or, for that matter, as a disturbed one either. It is a state of intelligence that questions our life and the meaning of life. It is the foundation of a search. A lot of things haven't been answered in our life—and we are still searching for the questions. That questioning is buddha nature. It is a state of potential. The more dissatisfaction, the more questions and more doubts there are, the healthier it is, for we are no longer sucked into ego-oriented situations, but we are constantly woken up.

86

THE SENSITIVITY
OF THE WARRIOR

IF THE warrior does not feel alone and
sad, then he or she can be corrupted very
easily. In fact, such a person may not be a
warrior at all. To be a good warrior, one has
to feel sad and lonely, but rich and re-
sourceful at the same time. This makes the
warrior sensitive to every aspect of phenomena: to sights, smells, sounds, and feel-
ings. In that sense, the warrior is also an
artist, appreciating whatever goes on in the
world. Everything is extremely vivid. The
rustling of your armor or the sound of rain-
drops falling on your coat is very loud. The

fluttering of occasional butterflies around you is almost an insult, because you are so sensitive.

87

WISDOM CANNOT BE BORN FROM THEORY

WISDOM CANNOT be born from theory; it must be born from your actual state of mind, which is the working basis for all spiritual practice. The wisdom of dealing with situations as they are, and that is what wisdom is, contains tremendous precision that could not come from anywhere else but the physical situations of sight, smell, feeling, touchable objects, and sounds. The earthy situation of actual things as they are is the source of wisdom. You can become completely one with smell, with sight, with sound, and your knowledge about them ceases to exist; your knowledge becomes wisdom.

88

MAKING FRIENDS
WITH OTHERS

EXPANDING *MAITRI*, or loving-kindness, to others cuts the neurosis of wishful thinking, the idea that you should be a good person only. Maitri is *intelligent* friendliness that allows acceptance of your whole being. It doesn't exclude friend or enemy, father or mother. It does not matter whether you regard your father as a friend and your mother as an enemy, your brother as a friend and your sister as an enemy, your friend as a friend, your friend as an enemy, or your enemy as a friend. The whole situation becomes extraordinarily spacious and is suddenly workable. Maybe there is hope after all. It is delightful that you could make friends with your parents and yourself, make friends with your enemies and yourself. Something is beginning to break through. Maitri is actually becoming real rather than imaginary. It is real because we don't have any hypothesis about how a good person should be or how we should improve ourselves. It is no longer hypothetical—it is real. Relationships exist; love and hate exist. Because they exist, therefore, we are able to work with them as stepping-stones. We begin to feel that we can afford to expand, that we can let go without protecting ourselves. We have developed enough maitri toward ourselves that we are no longer threatened by being open.

89

COMPASSION WITH
A THOUSAND ARMS

ONE OFTEN finds Avalokiteshvara, the great *bodhisattva* of compassion, portrayed as having a thousand arms and a thousand eyes, and these symbolize his innumerable activities. He took a vow to save all sentient beings. As long as there are more sentient beings and as long as there is more that needs to be done, his compassion also increases. And this shows that compassion is something within us. Where there is new suffering or a new outbreak of violence, that violence contains another eye, another hand of Avalokiteshvara. The two things always go together. There is always a kind of negative, but there is always a positive which comes with it. In this particular sense, then, one should not exclude the negative and work only for the positive, but realize that the negative contains the positive within itself. Therefore the act of compassion, the act of Avalokiteshvara, is never ending.

90

ENLIGHTENMENT IS IRRITATINGLY POSSIBLE

STUDENTS MIGHT find sanity too spacious, too irritating. We would prefer a little claustrophobic insanity, snug and comforting insanity. Getting into that is like crawling back into a marsupial's pouch. That's the usual tendency, because acknowledging precision and sanity is too crispy, too cool, too cold. It's too early to wake up; we'd rather go back to bed. Going back to bed is relating to the mind's deceptions, which in fact we prefer. We like to get a little bit confused and set up our homes in that. We don't prefer sanity or enlightenment in fact. That seems to be the problem rather than that we don't have it or can't get it. If we really prefer basic sanity or enlightenment, it's irritatingly possible to get into it.

PANORAMIC
AWARENESS

LIKE A great river that runs down toward the ocean, the narrowness of discipline leads into the openness of panoramic awareness. Meditation is not purely sitting alone in a particular posture attending to simple processes, but it is also an openness to the environment in which these processes take place. The environment becomes a reminder to us, continually giving us messages, teachings, insights.

LETTING GO

DON'T CONFUSE letting go with arrogance or indulgence. For the warrior,
letting go is relaxing within the discipline
you have already developed, in order to experience freedom. Letting go is not enjoying yourself at other people's expense,
promoting your ego and laying trips on
others. Arrogance of that kind is based on
fundamental insecurity, which makes you
insensitive rather than soft and gentle. The
confused, or setting-sun, version of letting
go is to take a drunken vacation or to
be wild and sloppy and do outrageous
things. For the warrior, rather than getting
away from the constraints of ordinary life,

letting go is going further into your life. You understand that your life, as it is, contains the means to unconditionally cheer you up.

93

SYNCHRONIZE
MIND AND BODY

WHEN YOU are completely mindful
in the present moment, mind and
body are synchronized. Here, synchronizing mind and body is connected with developing fearlessness, in the sense of being
accurate and direct in relating to the phenomenal world. That fearless vision reflects on you as well: it affects how you see
yourself. You begin to realize that you have
a perfect right to be in this universe. You
have looked and you have seen, and you
don't have to apologize for being born
on this earth. You can uplift yourself
and appreciate your existence as a human

being. This discovery is the first glimpse of what is called the Great Eastern Sun, which is the sun of human dignity, the sun of human power.

94

BASIC GOODNESS
IS LIKE A SNEEZE

WHEN WE talk about basic goodness, we are not talking in terms of good and bad, but we are talking about unconditional health or unconditional goodness, without any reference point. Basic goodness is something like a sneeze. When you sneeze, there is no time to create or refer to a reference point. You just sneeze, or you just cough. Similarly, when a person has an orgasm, there's no room or time to compare that experience with anything else. That simplicity and fundamental healthiness and that capability of having your own

personal experience is called basic goodness, which does not have to be compared
to basic badness.

95

MAKING FRIENDS
WITH THE
REAL WORLD

IN THE practice of meditation, having developed a sense of trust in oneself, slowly
that expands its expression outward, and
the world becomes a friendly world rather
than a hostile world. You could say that you
have changed the world: You have become
the king or queen of the universe. On the
other hand, you can't exactly say that, because the world has come toward you, to
return your friendship. It tried all kinds of
harsh ways to deal with you at the beginning, but finally the world and you begin
to speak with each other, and the world

becomes a real world, a completely real world, not at all an illusory world or a confused world. It is a real world. You begin to realize the reality of elements, the reality of time and space, the reality of emotions—the reality of everything.

96

THE VIEW FROM THE SUMMIT

THE TANTRIC journey is like walking along a winding mountain path. Dangers, obstacles, and problems occur constantly. There are wild animals, earthquakes, landslides, all kinds of things, but still we continue on our journey and we are able to go beyond the obstacles. When we finally get to the summit of the mountain, we do not celebrate our victory. Instead of planting our national flag on the summit of the mountain, we look down again and see a vast perspective of mountains, rivers, meadows, woods, jungles, and plains. Once we are on the summit of the mountain, we begin to look down, and we feel attracted toward the panoramic quality of what we see. That is *ati,* or ultimate, style. From that point of view, our achievement is not regarded as final but as a reappreciation of what we have already gone through. In fact, we would like to retake the journey we have been through.

97

FULL MOON IN
YOUR HEART

THE TEACHER, or the spiritual friend, enters your system much as medicine is injected into your veins. According to the tradition, this is known as planting the heart of enlightenment. It is transplanting the full moon into your heart. Can you imagine the full moon coming through your living room window and coming closer and suddenly entering your heart? On the one hand, unless you are terribly resentful, usually it is a tremendous relief: "Phew. The full moon has entered my heart." That's great, wonderful. On the other hand, however, when that particular full moon has entered into your heart, when it's transplanted into your heart, you might have a little panic. "Good heavens, what have I done? There's a moon in my heart. What am I going to do with it? It's too shiny!" By the way, once that moon has entered your heart, it cannot be a waning moon. It never wanes. It is always waxing.

98

BELIEVE IN YOUR BASIC GOODNESS

You don't have to feel inadequate; you just have to be. In order to do that, you need to develop an attitude of believing in your basic goodness and you need to practice meditation. When you sit like the Buddha, you begin to realize something called enlightenment. That is just realizing that there is something very straightforward and very sparkling in you. It is not necessarily feeling good. It is much better than feeling good; you have a sense of tremendous buoyancy, upliftedness. You feel healthy and simple and strong.

99

THE WISDOM
OF SHAMBHALA

THE BEST doctor of all the doctors, the best medicine of medicines, and the best technology of technologies cannot save you from your life. The best consultants, the best bank loans, and the best insurance policies cannot save you. Technology, financial help, your smartness or good thinking of any kind—none will save you. That may seem like the dark truth, but it is the real truth. In the Buddhist tradition, this is called the *vajra* truth, the diamond truth, the truth you cannot avoid or destroy.

We cannot avoid our lives at all—young

or old, rich or poor. Whatever happens, we cannot save ourselves from our lives at all. We have to face the truth—not even the eventual truth but the real truth of our lives. We are here; therefore, we have to learn how to go forward with our lives. This truth is what we call the wisdom of Shambhala.

TRUE PATIENCE

PATIENCE, *kshanti* in Sanskrit, is usually taken to mean forbearance and the calm endurance of pain and hardship. But in fact, it means rather more than that. It is forbearing in the sense of seeing the situation and seeing that it is right to forbear and to develop patience. *Kshanti* has an aspect of intelligence, in contrast, one might say, to an animal loaded with baggage who must go on and on walking along the track until it just drops dead.

That kind of patience is patience without wisdom, without clarity. In meditation, we develop patience with clarity, and energy with the eye of understanding.

INTRINSIC JOY

A LOT of us feel attacked by our own aggression and by our own misery and pain. But none of that particularly presents an obstacle to creating enlightened society. What we need, to begin with, is to develop kindness toward ourselves and then to develop kindness toward others. It sounds very simple-minded, which it is. At the same time, it is very difficult to practice.

Pain causes a lot of chaos and resentment, and we have to overcome that. It is an extremely simple logic. Once we can overcome pain, we discover intrinsic joy, and we have less resentment toward the world and ourselves. By being here, naturally being here, we have less resentment.

Resentment is not being here. We are somewhere else, because we are preoccupied with something else. When we are here, we are simply here—without resentment and without preoccupation. And by being here, we become cheerful.

SMILE AT FEAR

WHEN YOU are frightened by something, you have to relate with fear, explore why you are frightened, and develop some sense of conviction. You can actually look at fear. Then fear ceases to be the dominant situation that is going to defeat you. Fear can be conquered. You can be free from fear if you realize that fear is not the ogre. You can step on fear, and therefore you can attain what is known as fearlessness. But that requires that, when you see fear, you smile.

103

WORK WITH THE
PRESENT SITUATION

THE BUDDHIST tradition teaches the truth of impermanence, or the transitory nature of things. The past is gone and the future has not yet happened, so we work with what is here—the present situation. This actually helps us not to categorize or theorize. A fresh, living situation is taking place all the time, on the spot. This noncategorical approach comes from being fully here, rather than trying to reconnect with past events. We don't have to look back to the past in order to see what people are made out of. Human beings speak for themselves, on the spot.

GIVING A PART
OF ONESELF

YOU HAVE to be fully involved; you have to become one with what you are doing. So it is with giving things away. No matter how small the thing is in terms of value, one must be fully involved in the giving, so that a part of one's ego is also given away. Through that one reaches the *paramita*, the transcendental act, of generosity, which is something beyond the ordinary. If one is able to give *out* one's self, ego, a part of that possessiveness and passion, then one is really practicing the dharma, the teaching of the Buddha, which is passionlessness.

BUDDHA WASN'T
A BUDDHIST

HELPING OTHERS is a question of being genuine and projecting that genuineness to others. This way of being doesn't have to have a title or a name particularly. It is just being ultimately decent. Take the example of the Buddha himself— he wasn't a Buddhist!

BE THERE ALL ALONG

SOMETIMES PEOPLE find that being tender and raw is threatening and seemingly exhausting. Openness seems demanding and energy consuming, so they prefer to cover up their tender heart. Vulnerability can sometimes make you nervous. It is uncomfortable to feel so real, so you want to numb yourself. You look for some kind of anesthetic, anything that will provide you with entertainment. Then you can forget the discomfort of reality. People don't want to live with their basic rawness for even fifteen minutes. For the warrior, fearlessness is the opposite of that approach. Fearlessness is a question of learning how to be. Be there all along: that is the message. That is quite challenging in what we call the setting-sun world, the world of neurotic comfort where we use everything to fill up the space.

EMBRYONIC SADNESS

WHEN YOU are trying to help others, you begin to feel that the world is so disordered. I personally feel sadness, always. You feel sad, but you don't really want to burst into tears. You feel embryonic sadness. That sadness is a key point. In the back of your head, you hear a beautiful flute playing, because you are so sad. At the same time, the melody cheers you up. You are not on the bottom of the barrel of the world or in the Black Hole of Calcutta. In spite of being sad and devastated, there is something lovely taking place. There is some smile, some beauty. In the Shambhala world, we call that daringness. In the Buddhist language, we call it compassion.

Daringness is sympathetic to oneself. There is no suicidal sadness involved at all. Rather, there is a sense of big, open mind in dealing with others, which is beautiful, wonderful.

1 0 8

SIT AND DO NOTHING

THE WORLD can be explored; it is workable, wherever you go, whatever you do. But I would like to plant one basic seed in your mind: I feel that it is absolutely important to make the practice of meditation your source of strength, your source of basic intelligence. Please think about that. You could just sit down and do nothing. Stop acting, stop speeding. Sit and do nothing. You should take pride in the fact that you have learned a very valuable message: You actually can survive beautifully by doing nothing.

SOURCES

1. From "Discovering Basic Goodness," in *Shambhala: The Sacred Path of the Warrior,* Shambhala Library ed., 21.   2. From "Nowness," in *Shambhala: The Sacred Path of the Warrior,* 91. 3. From Talk One of *Warriorship in the Three Yanas.*   4. From Talk One of *Warriorship in the Three Yanas.*   5. From "The Cosmic Sneeze," in *Great Eastern Sun: The Wisdom of Shambhala,* 54.   6. From "The Life and Example of Buddha," in *Meditation in Action,* 1970 ed., 12–13. 7. From "The Development of Ego," in *Cutting Through Spiritual Materialism,* 121–22.   8. From "The Birth of Ego," in *The Sanity We Are Born With: A Buddhist Approach to Psychology,* 79–80.   9. From "Buddha Is Everywhere," in *Glimpses of Realization: The Three Bodies of*

Enlightenment, 72–73. 10. From "The Ultimate Truth Is Fearless."

11. From "Practice and Basic Goodness: A Talk to Children," in *The Heart of the Buddha*, 193–94. 12. From "Trapping the Monkey," in *The Teacup and the Skullcup: Chögyam Trungpa on Zen and Tantra*, 72. 13. From "The True Spiritual Path," in *The Essential Chögyam Trungpa*, 46. 14. From "What Is the Heart of the Buddha?" in *The Heart of the Buddha*, 6. 15. From "Fear and Fearlessness," in *Shambhala: The Sacred Path of the Warrior*, Shambhala Library ed., 36–37. 16. From "The Fourth Moment," in *Shambhala Sun* 14, no. 4 (March 2006): 43. 17. "From "Taming the Horse, Riding the Mind," in *The Sanity We Are Born With: A Buddhist Approach to Meditation*, 16. 18. From "Boredom," in *The Myth of Freedom and the Way of Meditation*, Shambhala Library ed., 70–71. 19. From "Fantasy and Reality," in *The Myth of Freedom and the Way of Meditation*, Shambhala Library ed., 3–4. 20. From "Maitri Space Awareness in a Buddhist Therapeutic

Community," in *The Sanity We Are Born With: A Buddhist Approach to Psychology,* 166.

21. From "Anuttara Yoga," in *Journey without Goal: The Tantric Wisdom of the Buddha,* 125. 22. From "The Basic Body," in *The Lion's Roar: An Introduction to Tantra,* 48. 23. From "A Golden Buddha," in *Glimpses of Mahayana* 12–13. 24. From "Working with Early Morning Depression," in *Great Eastern Sun: The Wisdom of Shambhala,* 27. 25. From "Disappointment," in *The Myth of Freedom and the Way of Meditation,* 5. 26. From "Creating an Enlightened Society," in *Shambhala: The Sacred Path of the Warrior,* 25–27. 27. From "Renunciation and Daring," in *Shambhala: The Sacred Path of the Warrior,* Shambhala Library ed., 63. 28. From "A New Year's Message." 29. From "Conquering Fear," in *The Collected Works of Chögyam Trungpa,* 8:396. 30. From "The Fool," in *The Myth of Freedom and the Way of Meditation,* 44.

31. From "How to Rule," in *Shambhala: The Sacred Path of the Warrior,* 119–20. 32. From

"An Approach to Meditation: A Talk to Psychologists," in *The Sanity We Are Born With: A Buddhist Approach to Psychology,* 55. 33. From "From a Workshop on Psychotherapy," in *The Sanity We Are Born With: A Buddhist Approach to Psychology,* 179. 34. From Talk One of *Work, Sex, and Money.* 35. From "Disappointment," in *Tibet Journal* 2, no. 4 (Winter 1977), 38. 36. From Talk Five of *Warriorship in the Three Yanas.* 37. From "Vajra Nature," in *Journey without Goal: The Tantric Wisdom of the Buddha,* 26. 38. From "The Path of Meditation," in *Karma,* 31–32. 39. From "Maha Ati," in *Journey without Goal: The Tantric Wisdom of the Buddha,* 138–39. 40. From "Ultimate and Relative Bodhichitta," in *Training the Mind and Cultivating Loving-Kindness* 11–12.

41. From Talk Five of *Warriorship in the Three Yanas.* 42. From "The Six Realms of Being," in *Transcending Madness: The Experience of the Six Bardos,* 51. 43. From "Ultimate and Relative Bodhichitta," in *Training the Mind and Cultivating Loving-Kindness,* 14–15. 44. From "Sudden Glimpse," in *Glimpses of Mahayana,* 36, 38–39.

45. From "From Raw Eggs to Stepping-Stones" in *The Path Is the Goal: A Basic Handbook of Buddhist Meditation*, 116.   46. From "How to Cultivate the Great Eastern Sun," in *Great Eastern Sun: The Wisdom of Shambhala*, 109–10.   47. From "Synchronizing Mind and Body," in *Shambhala: The Sacred Path of the Warrior*, Shambhala Library ed., 42–43.   48. From "The Basic Body," in *The Lion's Roar: An Introduction to Tantra*, 46.   49. From "Buddha Is Everywhere," in *Glimpses of Realization: The Three Bodies of Enlightenment*, 73.   50. From "Blamelessness: How to Love Yourself," in *Great Eastern Sun: The Wisdom of Shambhala*, 122–23.

51. From "The Bodhisattva Vow," in 1979 *Hinayana-Mahayana Seminary*, 80.   52. From "The Origins of Suffering," in 1975 *Hinayana-Mahayana Seminary*, 57.   53. From "Egolessness," in *The Myth of Freedom and the Way of Meditation*, Shambhala Library ed., 21.   54. From "The Wheel of Life," in *The Collected Works of Chögyam Trungpa*, 3:483.   55. From "Just the Facts," in *Elephant*, Summer 2007,

32. 56. From "Simplicity," in *The Myth of Freedom and the Way of Meditation*, 44–45. 57. From "The True Spiritual Path," in *The Essential Chögyam Trungpa*, 46. 58. From "The Tantric Journey," in *Journey without Goal: The Tantric Wisdom of the Buddha*, 122–23. 59. From "The True Spiritual Path," in *The Essential Chögyam Trungpa*, 46–47. 60. From "Discipline in the Four Seasons," in *Great Eastern Sun: The Wisdom of Shambhala*, 63.

61. From *Shambhala: The Sacred Path of the Warrior Book and Card Set*. 62. From "How to Invoke Magic," in *Shambhala: The Sacred Path of the Warrior*, 108–9. 63. From "Auspicious Coincidence," in *Glimpses of Abhidharma*, Shambhala Dragon ed., 99–100. 64. From "The Martial Arts and the Art of War," in *The Collected Works of Chögyam Trungpa*, 8:413–14. 65. From "The Meeting of Buddhist and Western Psychology," in *The Sanity We Are Born With: A Buddhist Approach to Psychology*, 10. 66. From "Creating an Environment of Sanity," in *The Sanity We Are Born With: A Buddhist Approach to Psychology*, 148–49. 67. From

"The Big No," in *Great Eastern Sun: The Wisdom of Shambhala*, 141. 68. From "Foreword" to *The Superhuman Life of Gesar of Ling*, in *The Collected Works of Chögyam Trungpa*, 8:408. 69. From "Ultimate and Relative Bodhichitta," in *Training the Mind and Cultivating Loving-Kindness*, 1993 ed., 16–17. 70. From "Dome Darshan" in *The Collected Works of Chögyam Trungpa*, 3:546.

71. From "Is Meditation Therapy?" in *The Sanity We Are Born With: A Buddhist Approach to Psychology*, 184–86. 72. From "The Four Foundations of Mindfulness," in *The Heart of the Buddha*, 46. 73. From "Recollecting the Present," in *The Path Is the Goal: A Basic Handbook of Buddhist Meditation*, 81–82. 74. From "The Way of the Buddha" in *The Myth of Freedom and the Way of Meditation*, 57–58. 75. From "The Meeting of Buddhist and Western Psychology," *The Sanity We Are Born With: A Buddhist Approach to Psychology*, 7. 76. From "Foreword" to *The Superhuman Life of Gesar of Ling*, in *The Collected Works of Chögyam Trungpa*, 8:409. 77. From *The Warrior's Way*, 11. 78. From

"Cosmic Disaster," in *Glimpses of Realization: The Three Bodies of Enlightenment*, 14. 79. From "The Bodhisattva Vow" in *The Heart of the Buddha*, 108–9. 80. From "The Achievement of Enlightenment" in *1974 Hinayana-Mahayana Seminary*, 164.

81. From "Point Three: Transformation of Bad Circumstances" in *Training the Mind and Cultivating Loving-Kindness*, 1993 ed., 88–89. 82. From Talk Nine of *The Tibetan Buddhist Path*. 83. From "The Bodhisattva Vow," in *The Heart of the Buddha*, 113. 84. From "The Achievement of Enlightenment" in *1974 Hinayana-Mahayana Seminary*, 164. 85. From "Awakening Buddha Nature," in *Glimpses of Mahayana*, 19. 86. From "Conquering Fear," in *The Collected Works of Chogyam Trungpa*, 8:400–401. 87. From "Form," in *Glimpses of Abhidharma*, 12. 88. From "Awakening Buddha Nature," in *Glimpses of Mahayana*, 21–22. 89. From "The Mahasattva Avalokiteshvara," in *The Collected Works of Chögyam Trungpa*, 1:450–51. 90. From "The Lion's Roar," in *Crazy Wisdom*, 142–43.

91. From "Fantasy and Reality," in *The Myth of Freedom and the Way of Meditation*, Shambhala Library ed., 6–7. 92. From *Shambhala: The Sacred Path of the Warrior Book and Card Set*. 93. From *Shambhala: The Sacred Path of the Warrior Book and Card Set*. 94. From "Natural Hierarchy," in *The Collected Works of Chögyam Trungpa*, 8:435. 95. From "Dynamic Stillness and Cosmic Absorption," in *The Teacup and the Skullcup: Chögyam Trungpa on Zen and Tantra*, 99. 96. From "Maha Ati," in *Journey without Goal: The Tantric Wisdom of the Buddha*, 133–34. 97. From Talk Two of *Warriorship in the Three Yanas*. 98. From "Practice and Basic Goodness: A Talk to Children," in *The Heart of the Buddha*, 193–94. 99. From "Save Yourself," in *Elephant*, Spring 2007, 30. 100. From "Patience," in *Meditation in Action*, Shambhala Pocket Classic ed., 85.

101. From "A Question of Heart," in *Great Eastern Sun: The Wisdom of Shambhala*, 191–92. 102. From "Mirrorlike Wisdom," in *Great Eastern Sun: The Wisdom of Shambhala*, 75. 103. From "Becoming a Full Human Being,"

in *The Sanity We Are Born With: A Buddhist Approach to Psychology*, 139. 104. From "Generosity," in *Meditation in Action*, Shambhala Library ed., 63. 105. From "Becoming a Full Human Being," in *The Sanity We Are Born With: A Buddhist Approach to Psychology*, 142. 106. From "Conquering Fear," in *The Collected Works of Chögyam Trungpa*, 8:397. 107. From "Helping Others," in *Great Eastern Sun: The Wisdom of Shambhala*, 175–76. 108. From "Maha Ati," in *Journey without Goal: The Tantric Wisdom of the Buddha*, 142.

BIBLIOGRAPHY

BOOKS

The Collected Works of Chögyam Trungpa. Edited by Carolyn Rose Gimian. 8 vols. Boston: Shambhala, 2003 and 2004.

Crazy Wisdom. Edited by Sherab Chödzin. Boston: Shambhala, 1991.

Cutting Through Spiritual Materialism. Edited by John Baker and Marin Casper. Boston: Shambhala, 1973; Shambhala Classic ed., 2002; Shambhala Dragon ed., 1987.

The Essential Chögyam Trungpa. Edited by Carolyn Rose Gimian. Boston: Shambhala, 2000.

Glimpses of Abhidharma: From a Seminar on Buddhist Psychology. Boulder: Prajna, 1978; Shambhala Dragon ed., 1987.

Glimpses of Mahayana. Edited by Judith L. Lief. Halifax: Vajradhatu, 2001.

BIBLIOGRAPHY

Glimpses of Realization: The Three Bodies of Enlightenment. Edited by Judith L. Lief. Halifax: Vajradhatu, 2006.

Great Eastern Sun: The Wisdom of Shambhala. Edited by Carolyn Rose Gimian. Boston: Shambhala, 1999.

The Heart of the Buddha. Edited by Judith L. Lief. Boston: Shambhala, 1991.

Journey without Goal: The Tantric Wisdom of the Buddha. Edited by Carolyn Rose Gimian. Boston: Shambhala, 1981.

The Lion's Roar: An Introduction to Tantra. Edited by Sherab Chödzin. Boston: Shambhala, 1992.

Meditation in Action. Boston: Shambhala, 1969; Shamhala Pocket Classic ed., 1996; Shambhala Library ed., 2004.

The Myth of Freedom and the Way of Meditation. Edited by John Baker and Marin Casper. Boston: Shambhala, 1976; Shambhala Classic ed., 2002; Shambhala Dragon ed., 1988; Shambhala Library ed., 2005.

The Path Is the Goal: A Basic Handbook of Buddhist Meditation. Edited by Sherab Chödzin. Boston: Shambhala, 1995.

The Sanity We Are Born With: A Buddhist Approach to Psychology. Edited by Carolyn Rose Gimian. Boston: Shambhala, 2005.

Shambhala: The Sacred Path of the Warrior. Edited by Carolyn Rose Gimian. Boston: Shambhala, 1984; Shambhala Dragon ed., 1988; Shambhala Library ed., 2003.

The Teacup and the Skullcup: Chögyam Trungpa on Zen and Tantra. Edited by Judith L. Lief and David Schneider. Halifax: Vajradhatu, 2007.

Training the Mind and Cultivating Loving-Kindness. Edited by Judith L. Lief. Boston: Shambhala, 1993; Shambhala Library ed., 2005.

Transcending Madness: The Experience of the Six Bardos. Edited by Judith L. Lief. Boston: Shambhala, 1992.

OTHER SOURCES

"Disappointment." *Tibet Journal* 2, no. 4 (Winter 1977): 37–40.

"The Fourth Moment." *Shambhala Sun* 14, no. 4 (March 2006), 42–48, 92–95.

"Just the Facts." *Elephant,* Summer 2007, 32.

"A New Year's Message." Unpublished transcript of a talk delivered for the Tibetan New Year, 1981.

1974 Hinayana-Mahayana Seminary. Sourcebook. Halifax: Vajradhatu, 1975.

1975 Hinayana-Mahayana Seminary. Sourcebook. Halifax: Vajradhatu, 1976.

1979 Hinayana-Mahayana Seminary. Sourcebook. Halifax: Vajradhatu, 1980.

"Save Yourself." *Elephant,* Spring 2007, 30.

Shambhala: The Sacred Path of the Warrior Book and Card Set—53 Principles for Living Life with Fearlessness and Gentleness. Boston: Shambhala, 2004.

The Tibetan Buddhist Path. Unpublished transcript of a thirteen-talk seminar, Naropa Institute, Boulder, Colo., July 1974.

"The Ultimate Truth Is Fearless." Unpublished transcript of a talk. Boulder, Colorado, February 25, 1972.

The Warrior's Way. Sourcebook. Halifax: Vajradhatu, 1983.

Warriorship in the Three Yanas. Unpublished transcript of a five-talk seminar, Rocky Mountain Dharma Center, August 1978.

Work, Sex, and Money. Unpublished transcript of a three-talk seminar, Burlington, Vt., April 1972.

FURTHER READINGS
AND RESOURCES

BOOKS

The Sanity We Are Born With: A Buddhist Approach to Psychology is an excellent overview of Chögyam Trungpa's writings on the Buddhist view of mind, the practice of meditation, and the application of the Buddhist teachings to working with oneself and others in the field of psychology. Additional discussion of the practice of meditation overall and an in-depth treatment of mindfulness and awareness (*shamatha* and *vipashyana*) meditation is provided by Chögyam Trungpa in *The Path Is the Goal: A Basic Handbook of Buddhist Meditation*. The discussion of awareness practice is particularly well developed in this small manual on Buddhist practice.

Cultivating loving-kindness and compassion toward all beings is at the root of Chögyam Trungpa's approach to working with others. *Training the Mind and Cultivating Loving-Kindness* presents fifty-nine slogans, or aphorisms related to meditation practice, that show a practical path to making friends with oneself and developing compassion for others.

For readers interested in an overview of the Buddhist path, the following volumes are recommended: *Cutting Through Spiritual Materialism, The Myth of Freedom and the Way of Meditation,* and *The Essential Chögyam Trungpa.*

The Shambhala path of warriorship offers heartfelt advice on transforming fear and anxiety into gentle bravery, so that one develops confidence and skill in working with others. These teachings on basic goodness and how to be more self-assured, yet genuine and vulnerable, in one's life are available in *Shambhala: The Sacred Path of the Warrior* and *Great Eastern Sun: The Wisdom of Shambhala. Shambhala: The Sacred Path of the Warrior Book and Card Set* provides a small handbook and a group of slogan cards that can be used to contemplate these teachings on working with oneself and others.

OTHER RESOURCES

Ocean of Dharma Quotes of the Week brings you the teachings of Chögyam Trungpa Rinpoche. An e-mail is sent out several times each week containing a quote from Chögyam Trungpa's extensive teachings. Quotations of material may be from unpublished material, forthcoming publications, or previously published sources. Ocean of Dharma Quotes of the Week are selected by Carolyn Rose Gimian. To enroll, go to www.oceanofdharma.com.

For information regarding meditation instruction, please visit the Web site of Shambhala International at www.shambhala.org. This Web site contains information about the more than one hundred centers affiliated with Shambhala.

The Chögyam Trungpa Legacy Project is an independent nonprofit foundation being incorporated in the United States, in Canada (as a charitable organization), and eventually in Europe. It was established to help preserve, disseminate, and expand Chögyam Trungpa's legacy. The Legacy Project supports the preservation, propagation, and publication of Trungpa Rinpoche's dharma teachings. This includes plans for the creation of a comprehensive virtual archive and learning community. For information, go to http://ChogyamTrungpa.com

For publications from Vajradhatu Publications and Kalapa Recordings, including both books and audio-visual materials, go to www.shambhalashop.com.

For information about the archive of the author's work, please contact the Shambhala Archives: archives@shambhala.org.

ABOUT
CHÖGYAM TRUNGPA

BORN IN Tibet in 1939, Chögyam Trungpa was recognized in infancy as an important reincarnate teacher, or rinpoche. His was the last generation to receive the complete education in the teachings of Buddhism while in Tibet. The abbot of the Surmang Monasteries and the governor of the Surmang District of Eastern Tibet, Trungpa Rinpoche was forced to flee his homeland in 1959 to escape persecution by the communist Chinese. His harrowing journey over the Himalayas to freedom lasted ten months.

After several years in India, where he was the spiritual adviser to the Young Lamas School, Trungpa Rinpoche immigrated to England, where he studied at Oxford University and established the Samye Ling Meditation Centre in Scotland. Following a serious auto accident in 1969, which he regarded as a message to be more open and courageous, Trungpa Rinpoche gave up his monastic robes and became a lay teacher, in order to communicate more directly with Western students. In January 1970, he married Diana Judith Pybus and shortly thereafter immigrated to North America, where he remained until his death in Halifax, Nova Scotia, in 1987.

One of the first Tibetan lineage holders to present the Buddhist teachings in English, Chögyam Trungpa's command of the English language and his understanding of the Western mind made him one of the most important influences on the development of Buddhism in the West. He established hundreds of meditation centers throughout North America, founded Naropa University in Boulder, Colorado—the first Buddhist-inspired university in North America—and attracted several thousand committed students, who received advanced teachings from him and have continued to propagate his teachings and lineage in North America. Chögyam Trungpa was also instrumental in bringing many other great Tibetan lineage holders to teach in North America. In 1977, he established Shambhala Training, a program to present meditation and the Shambhala tradition of warriorship to a broad audience. The author of more than two dozen popular books on Buddhism, meditation, and the path of Shambhala warriorship, he was an ecumenical teacher who sought out the wisdom in other schools of Buddhism and in other religions. He also studied and promoted a contemplative awareness of the visual arts, design, poetry, theater, and other aspects of Western art and culture.

(continued on next page)